# Easy Piano Collection

ISBN 978-1-4950-0628-9

7777 W. BLUEMOUND RD. P.O. BOX 13819 MILWAUKEE, WI 53213

In Australia Contact:
**Hal Leonard Australia Pty. Ltd.**
4 Lentara Court
Cheltenham, Victoria, 3192 Australia
Email: ausadmin@halleonard.com.au

Visit Hal Leonard Online at
**www.halleonard.com**

# ANOTHER ONE BITES THE DUST

Words and Music by
JOHN DEACON

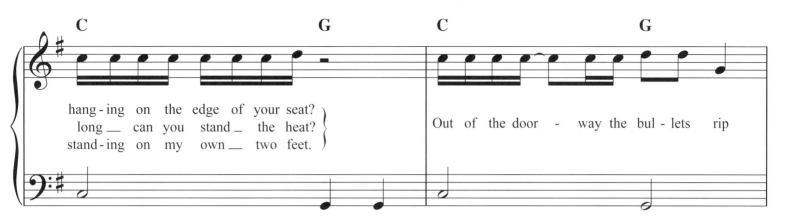

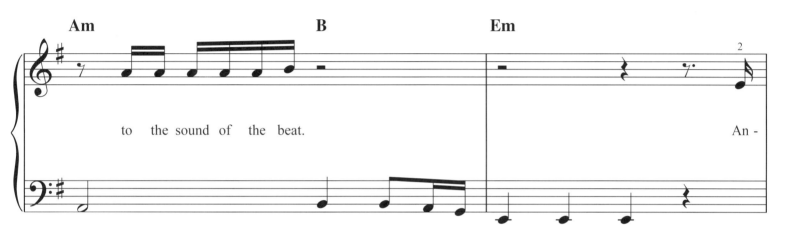

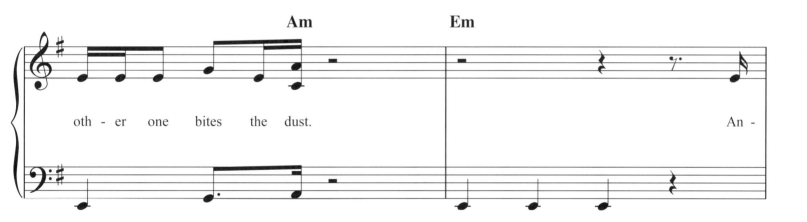

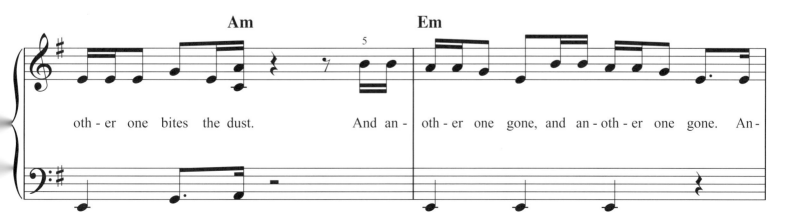

4

oth - er one bites the dust. Hey! I'm gon - na get you too. An-

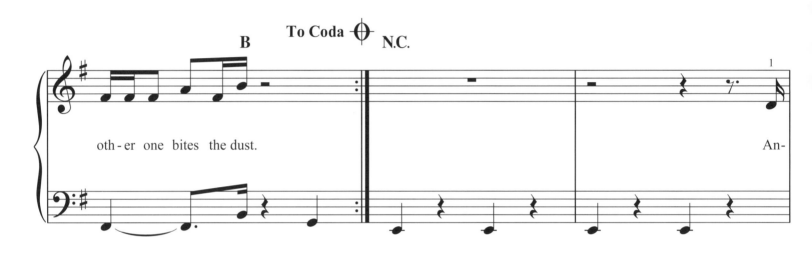

oth - er one bites the dust. An-

oth - er one bites the dust. An - oth - er one bites the dust. An -

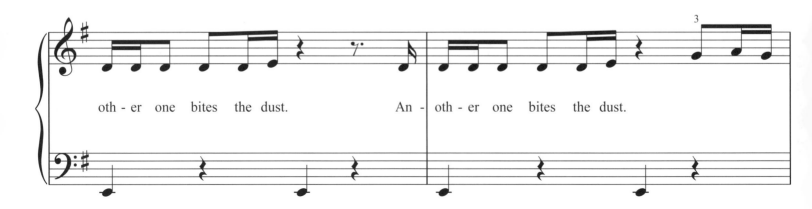

oth - er one bites the dust. An - oth - er one bites the dust.

# BOHEMIAN RHAPSODY

Words and Music by
FREDDIE MERCURY

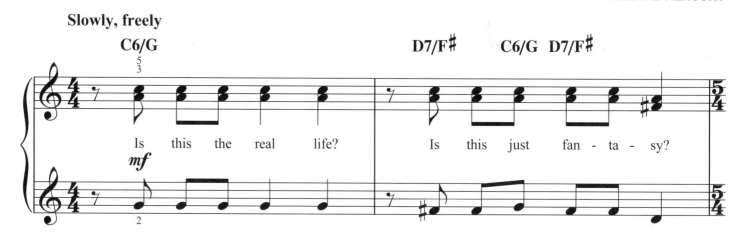

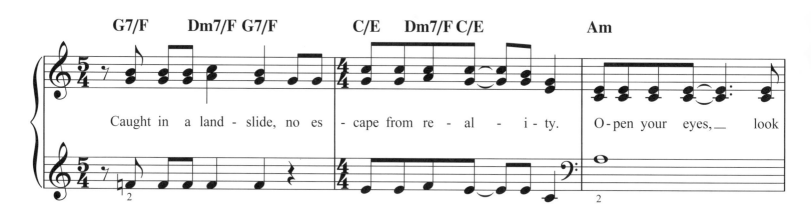

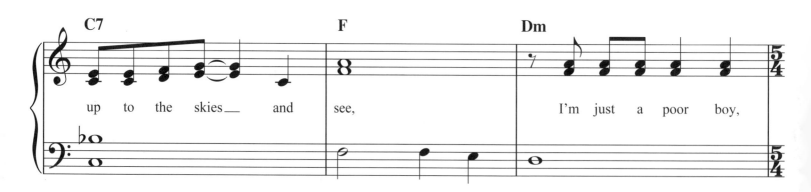

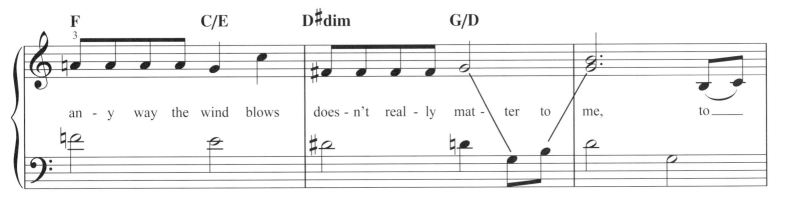

an-y way the wind blows does-n't real-ly mat-ter to me, to____

me.

**Slowly, steady tempo**

Ma - ma____ just
Too late,____ my

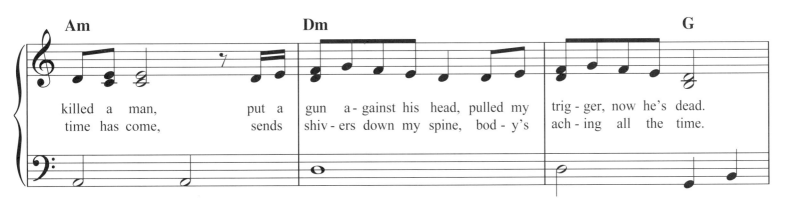

killed a man, put a gun a-gainst his head, pulled my trig-ger, now he's dead.
time has come, sends shiv-ers down my spine, bod-y's ach-ing all the time.

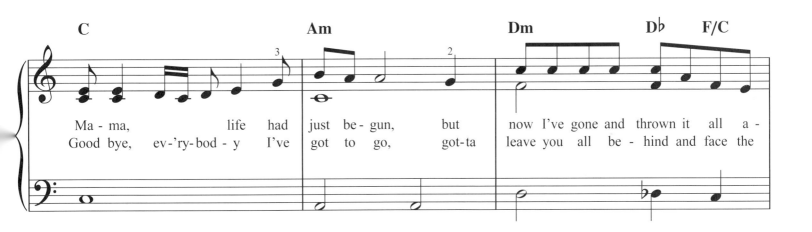

Ma - ma, life had just be-gun, but now I've gone and thrown it all a-
Good bye, ev-'ry-bod-y I've got to go, got-ta leave you all be-hind and face the

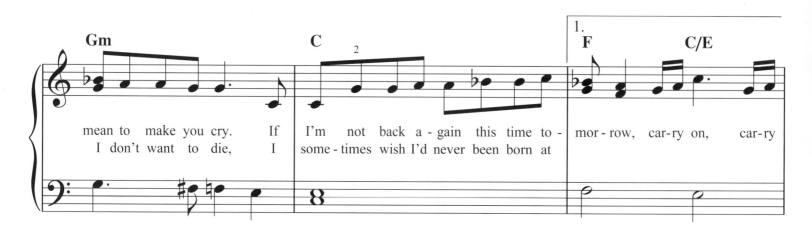

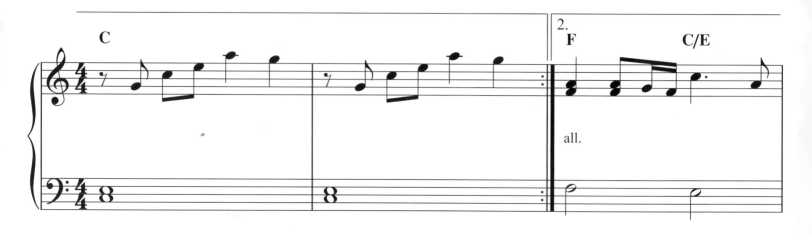

**Double Time (♪ = ♩)**

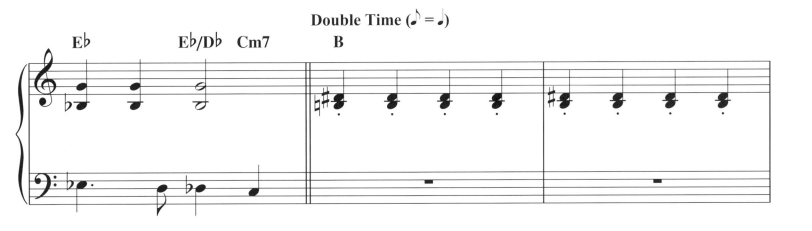

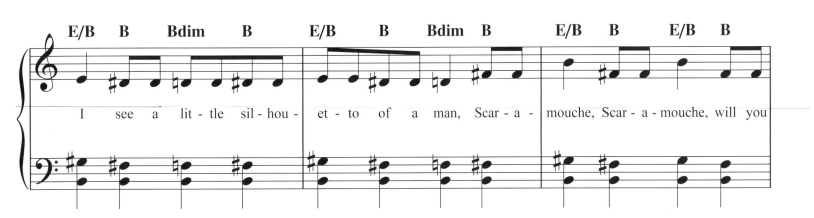

I see a lit - tle sil - hou - et - to of a man, Scar - a - mouche, Scar - a - mouche, will you

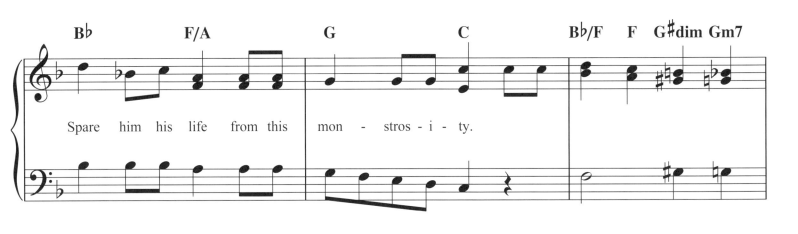

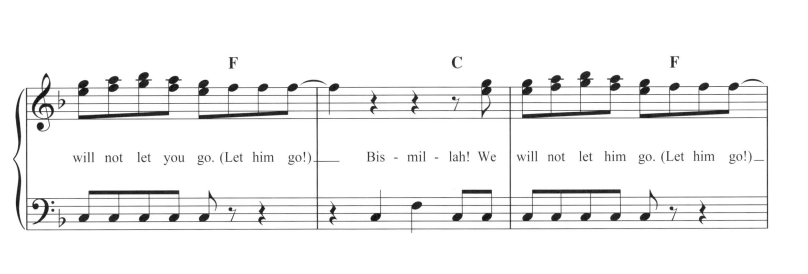

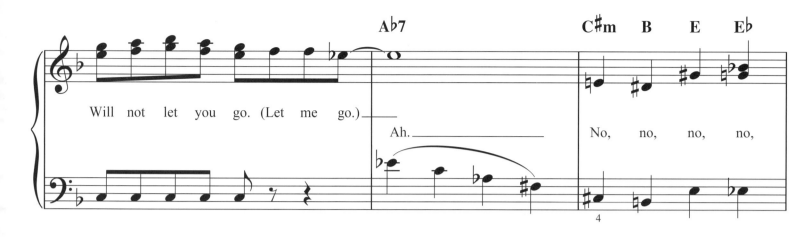

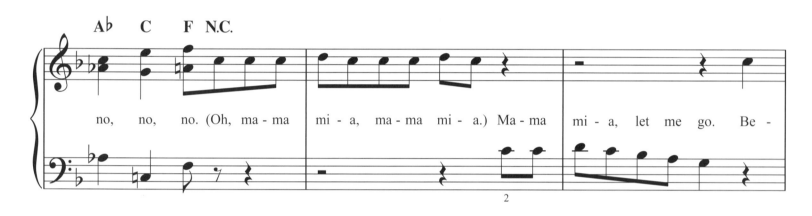

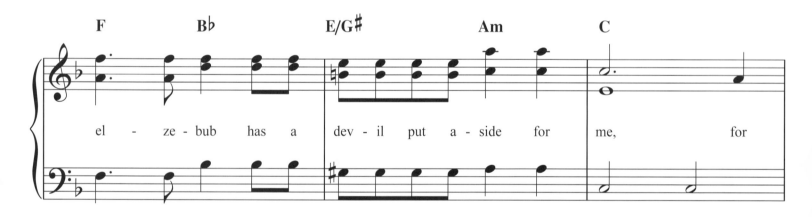

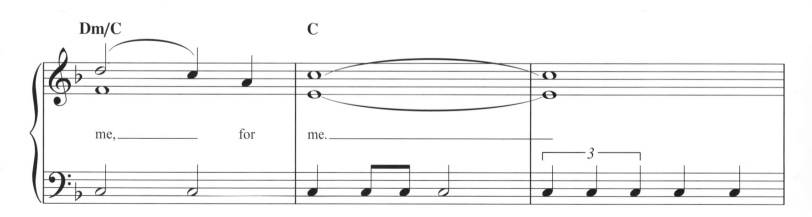

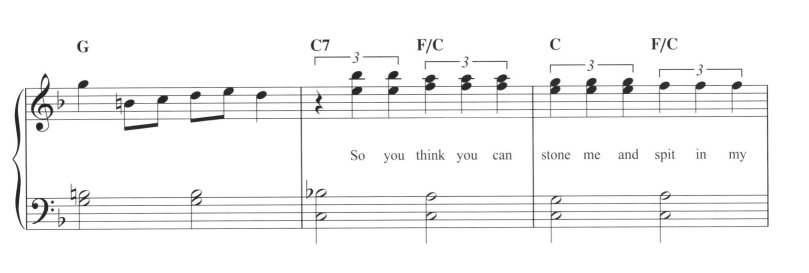

So you think you can stone me and spit in my

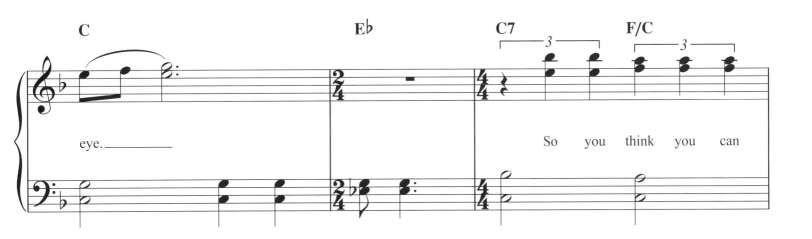

eye._____

So you think you can

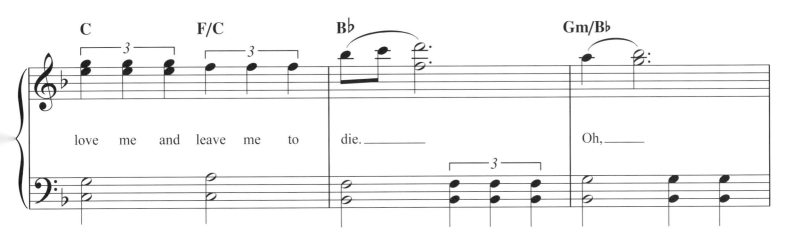

love me and leave me to die._____

Oh,_____

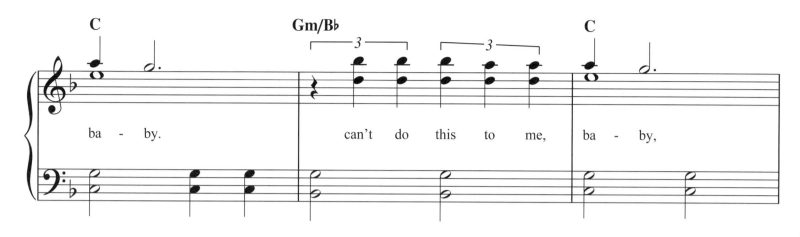

ba - by.   can't do this to me, ba - by,

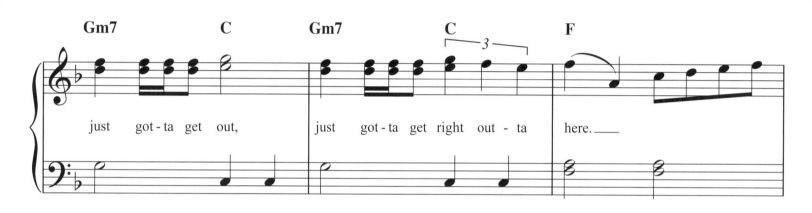

just got - ta get out,   just got - ta get right out - ta   here. ___

*rit.*

**Slowly, a tempo**

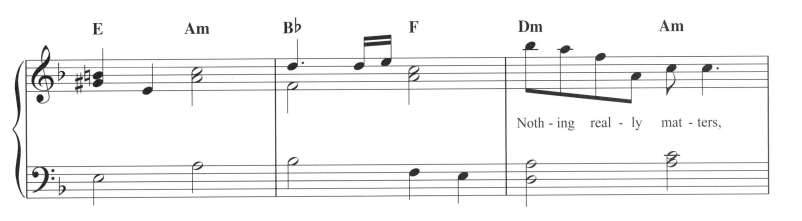

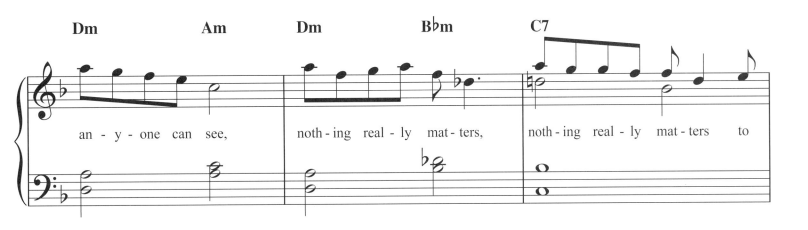

# CRAZY LITTLE THING CALLED LOVE

Words and Music by
FREDDIE MERCURY

love. Well, this thing— There goes my ba - by; —

she knows — how to rock and roll. — She drives — me cra - zy. —

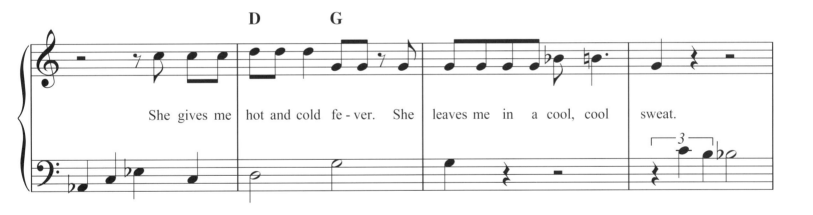

She gives me hot and cold fe - ver. She leaves me in a cool, cool sweat.

I got - ta be cool, —

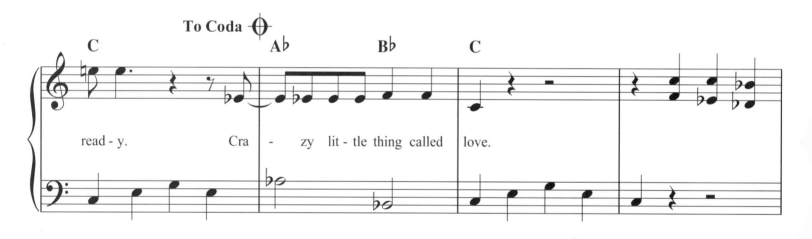

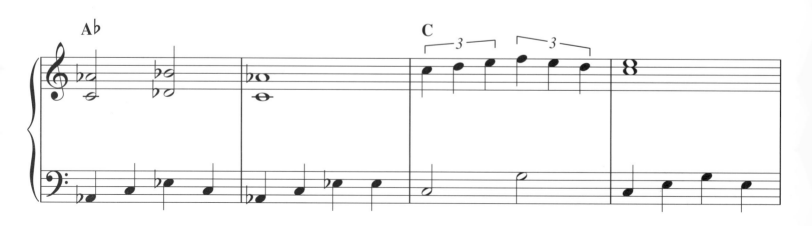

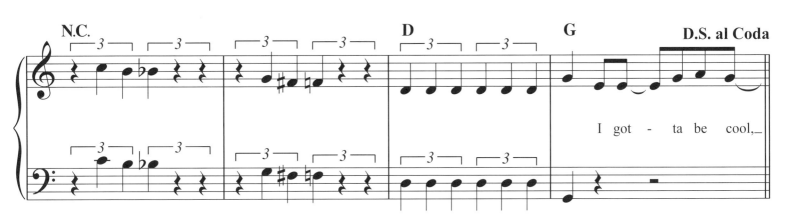

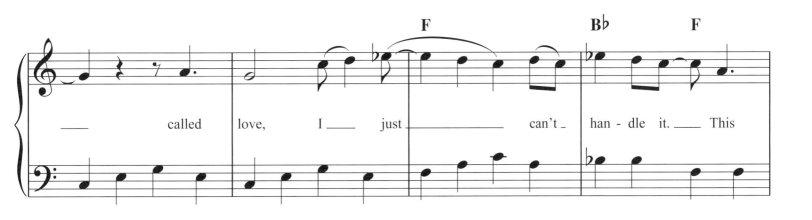

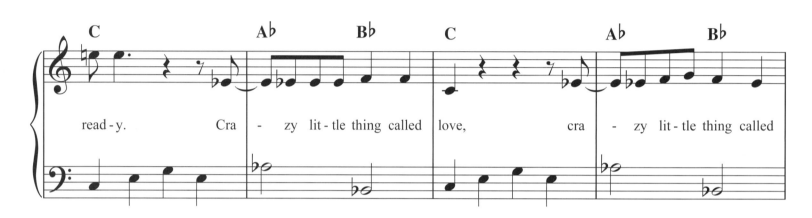

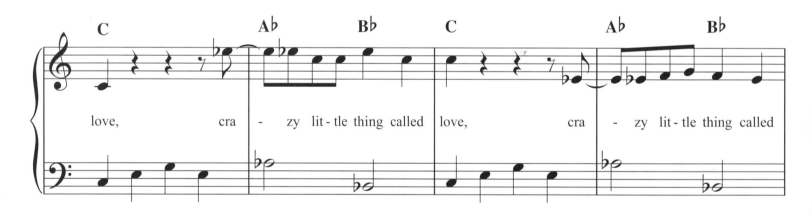

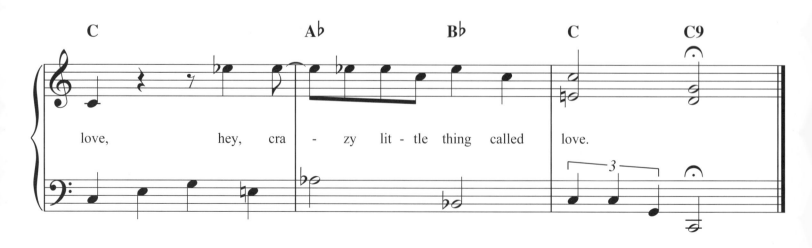

# DON'T STOP ME NOW

Words and Music by
FREDDIE MERCURY

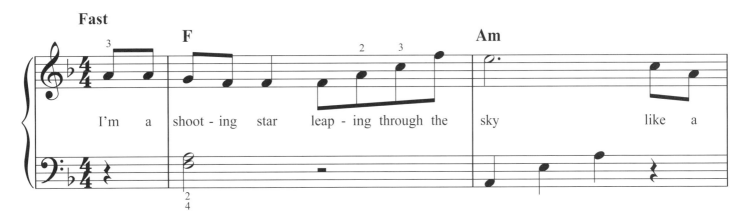

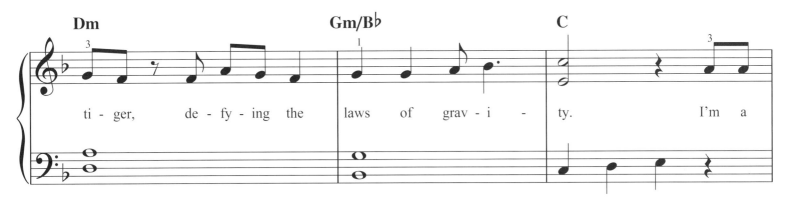

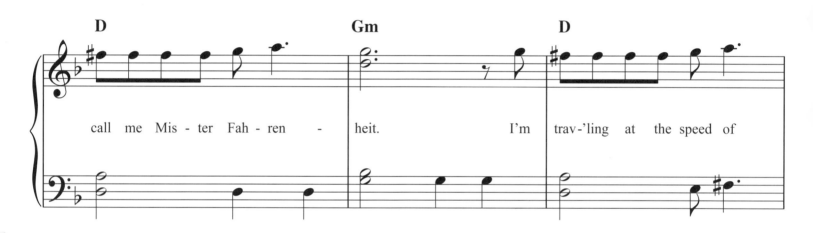

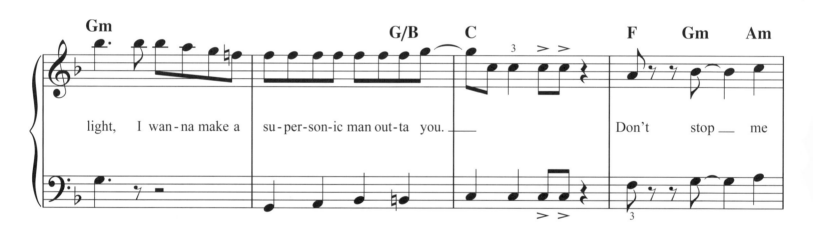

Don't stop __ me now, if you wan - na have a good time, just

give me a call. __ Don't stop me, 'cause I'm hav - ing a good __ time,

don't stop, yes I'm hav - ing a good __ time, I don't wan - na stop at

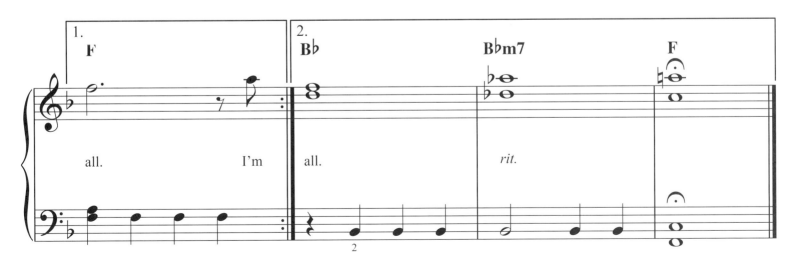

all.    I'm    all.    *rit.*    all.

# KILLER QUEEN

Words and Music by
FREDDIE MERCURY

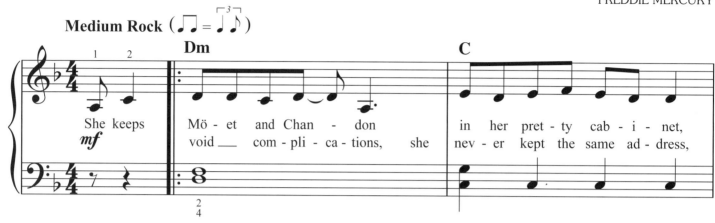

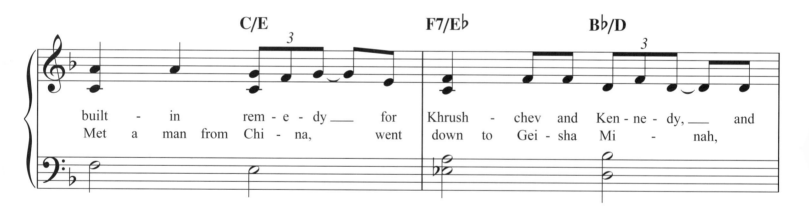

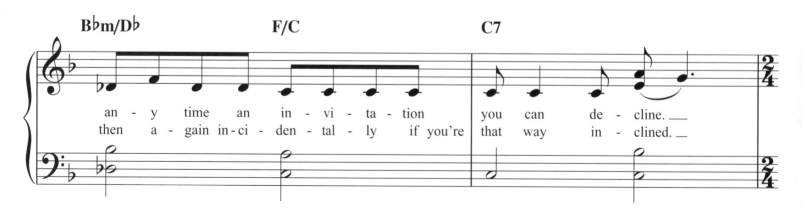

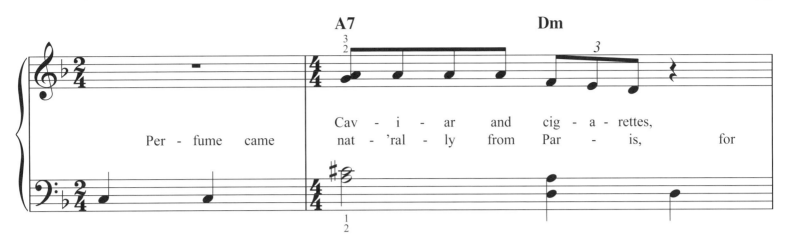

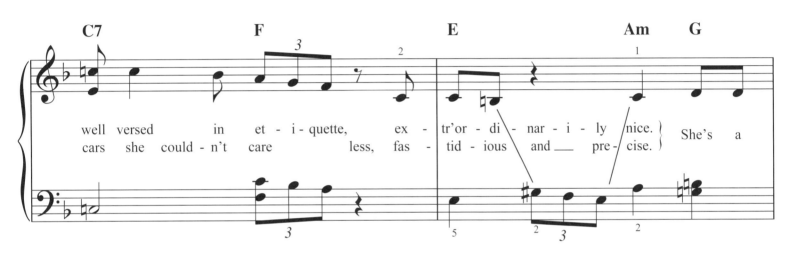

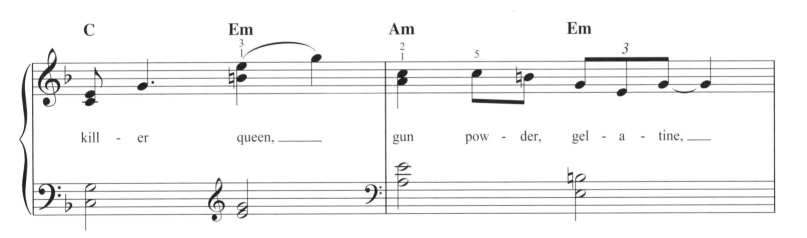

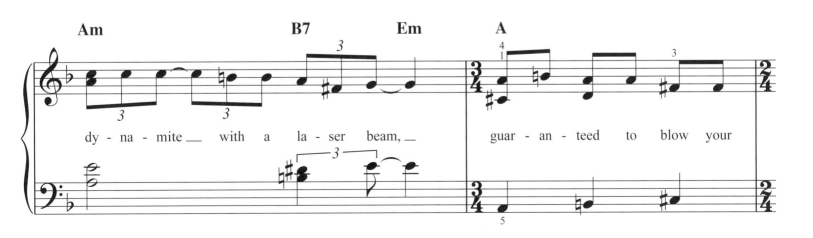

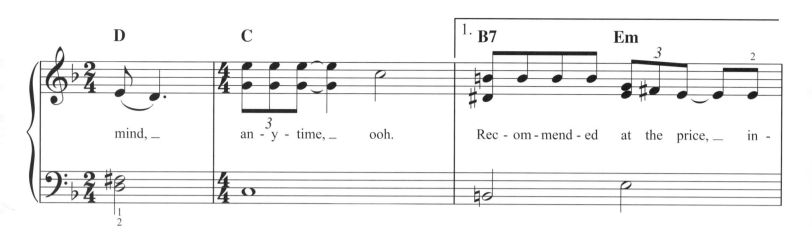

mind, _ an - y - time, _ ooh. Rec - om - mend - ed at the price, _ in -

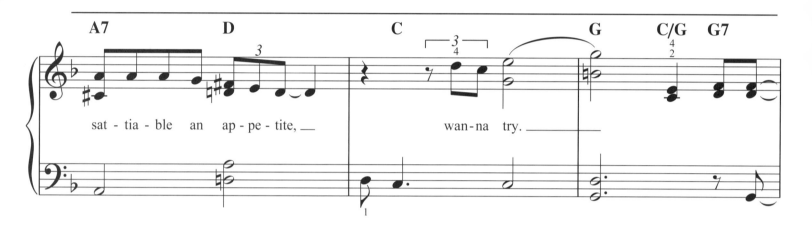

sat - tia - ble an ap - pe - tite, _ wan-na try. ____

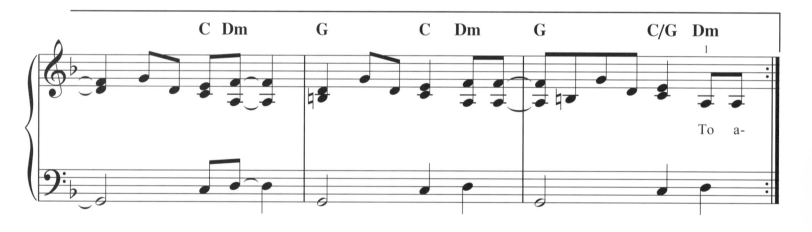

To a-

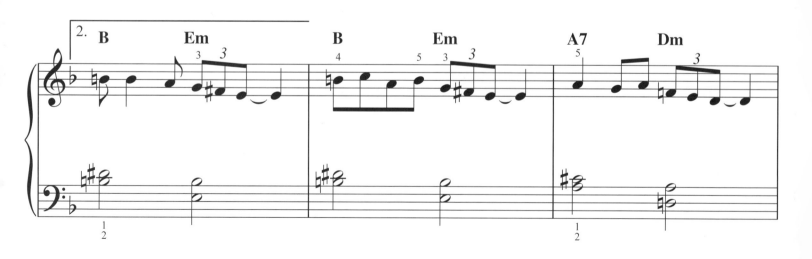

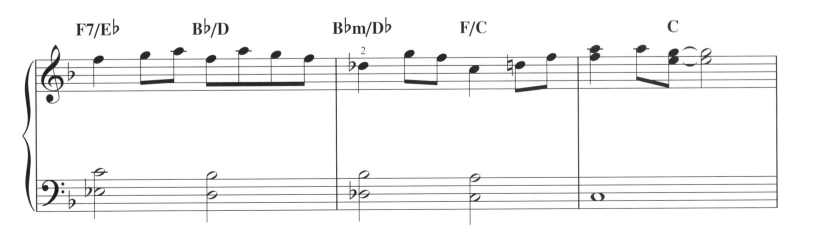

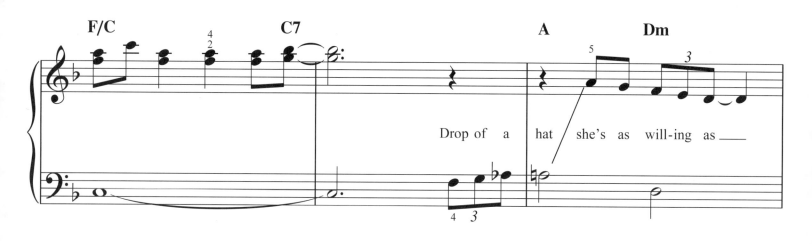

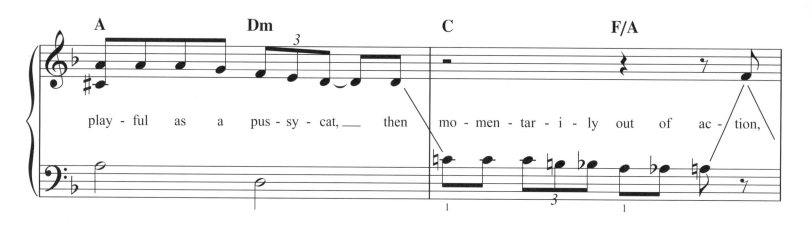

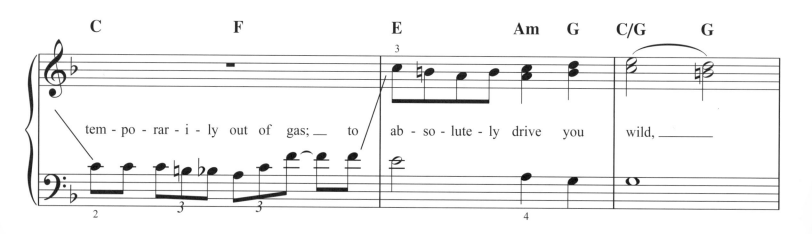

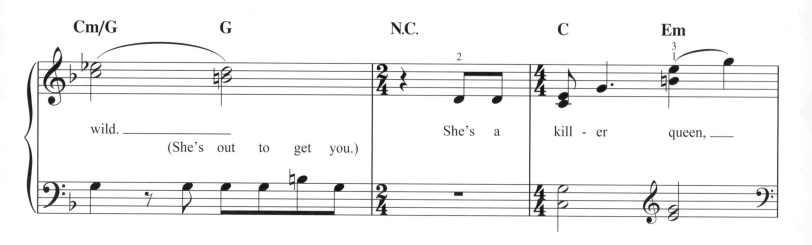

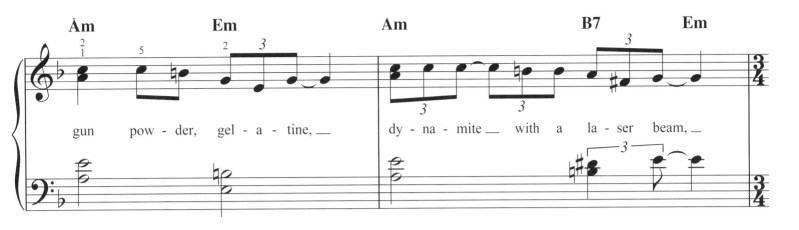

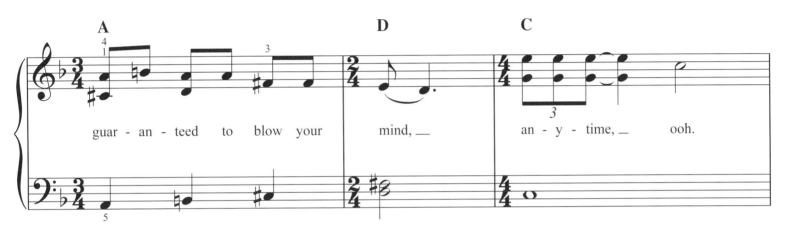

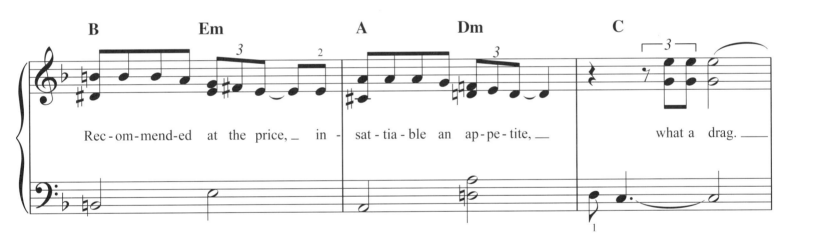

# SOMEBODY TO LOVE

Words and Music by
FREDDIE MERCURY

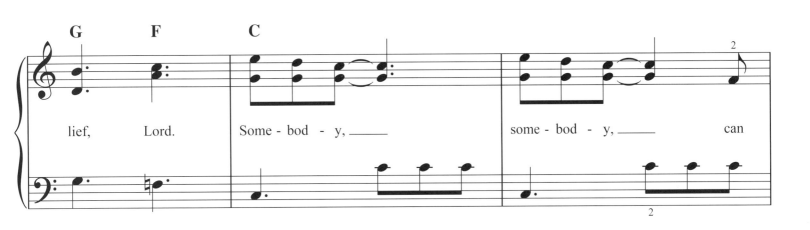

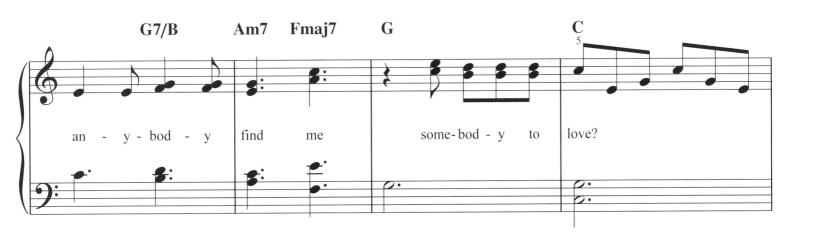

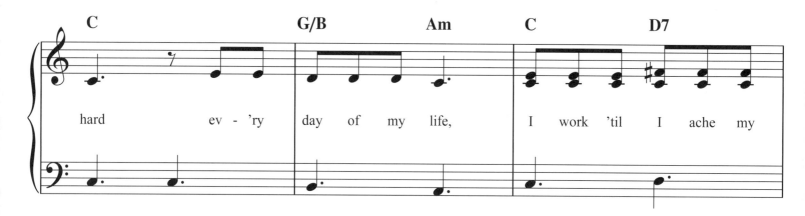

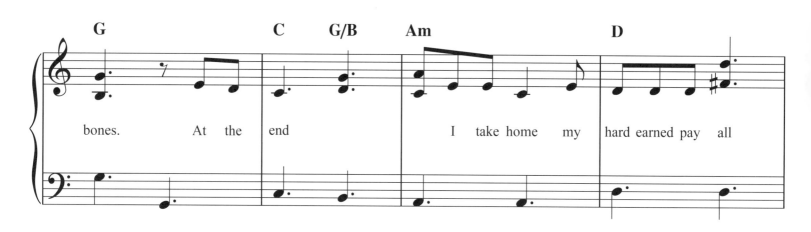

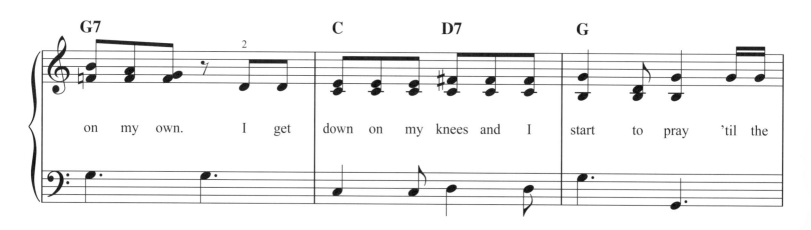

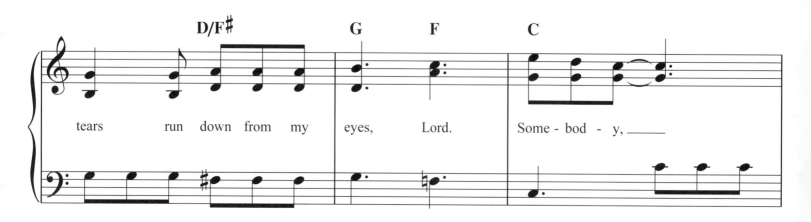

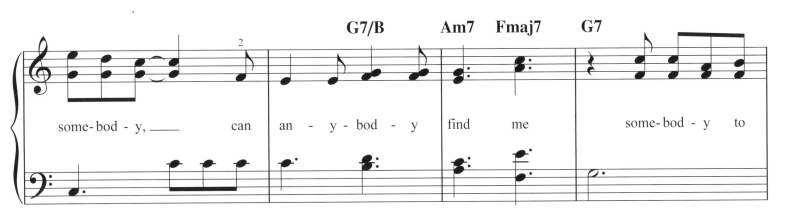

some-bod - y, _____ can an - y-bod - y find me somebod - y to

love?

Ev - 'ry _____ day I try and I try and I try, _____ but

ev - 'ry-bod - y wants to put me down, they say I'm go - in'

cra - zy. _____ They say I got a lot of wat-er in my brain, _____

got no com-mon sense. I got no - bod-y left to be - lieve. _____

Yeah, _____ yeah, _____ yeah, _____ yeah.

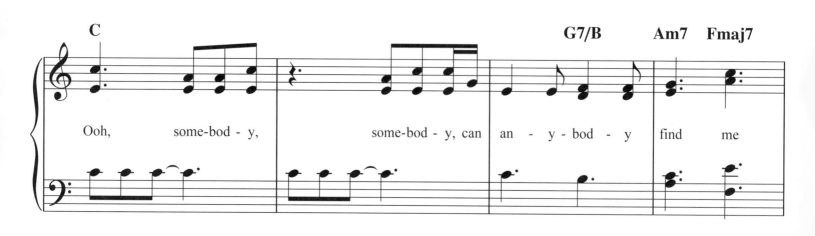

Ooh, some-bod - y, some-bod - y, can an - y-bod - y find me

some - bod - y to love? _____

Got no feel. I got no rhy - thm. I _____

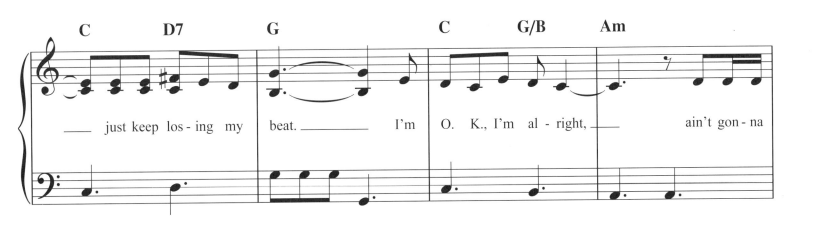

_____ just keep los - ing my beat. _____ I'm O. K., I'm al - right, _____ ain't gon - na

face _____ no de - feat. I just got - ta get out of this

find me some - bod - y to love, \_\_\_\_\_ love, \_\_\_\_\_ love. \_\_\_\_\_

Find me some - bod - y to love, \_\_\_\_\_ find me some -

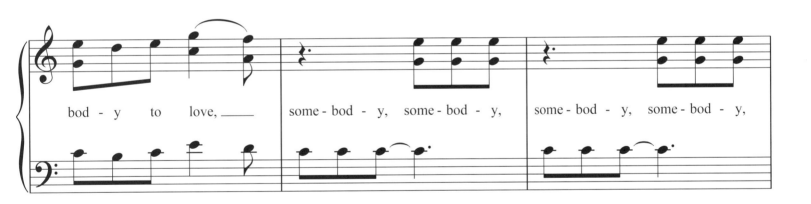

bod - y to love, \_\_\_\_\_ some - bod - y, some - bod - y, some - bod - y, some - bod - y,

some - bod - y. Find me some - bod - y, find me some - bod - y to love. Can

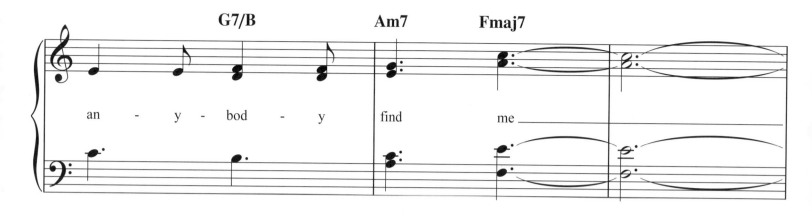

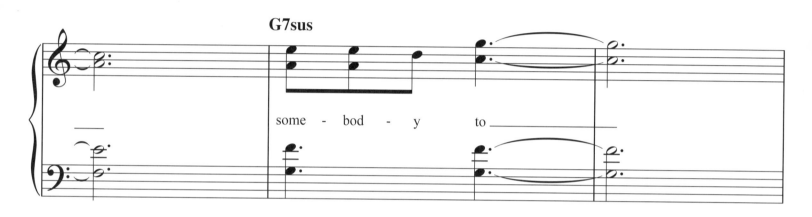

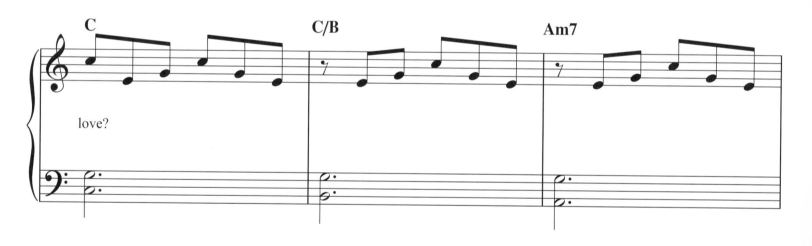

# UNDER PRESSURE

Words and Music by FREDDIE MERCURY,
JOHN DEACON, BRIAN MAY,
ROGER TAYLOR and DAVID BOWIE

Moderately

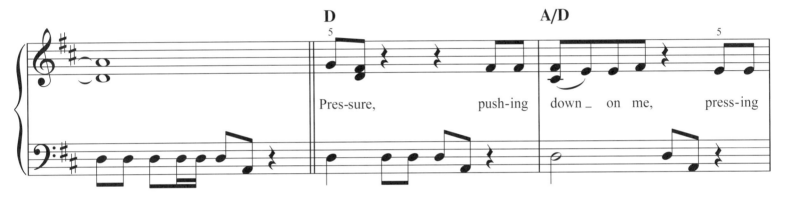

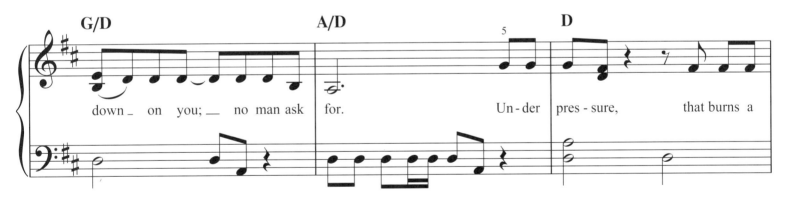

Bah bah bah, bah bah bah, bah bah bah, bah bah bah. It's the

ter - ror of know-ing what this world is a - bout, watch - ing some good friends scream-ing,

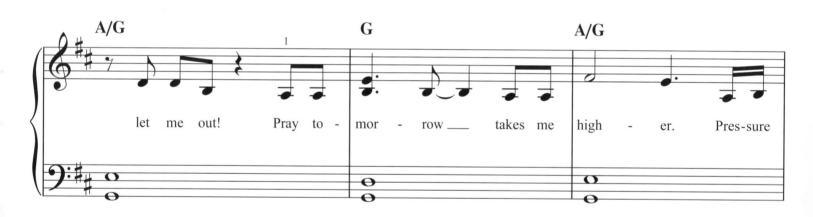

let me out! Pray to - mor - row ___ takes me high - er. Pres-sure

on peo - ple; peo-ple on streets. ___ Turned a - way from it all like a

blind man;    sat on a fence,    but it don't work.    Keep

com-ing up with love, but it's so   slashed and torn.   Why? _____    Why?    Why? _____

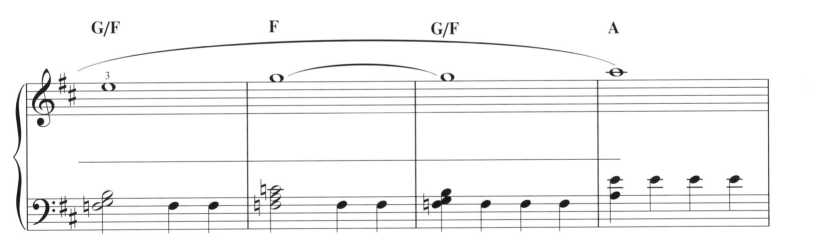

In - san - i - ty   laughs, _ un - der   pres-sure we're crack - ing. Can't we

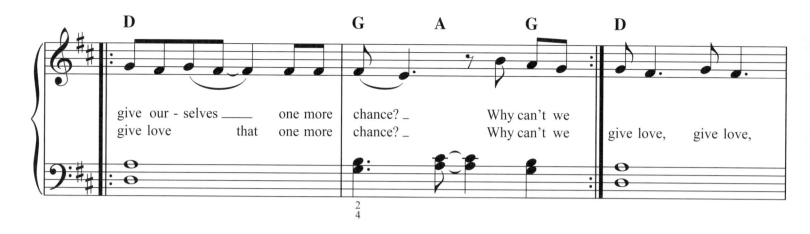

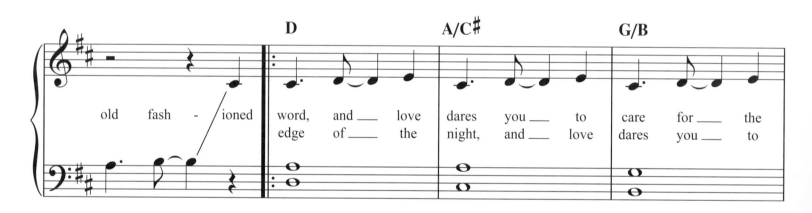

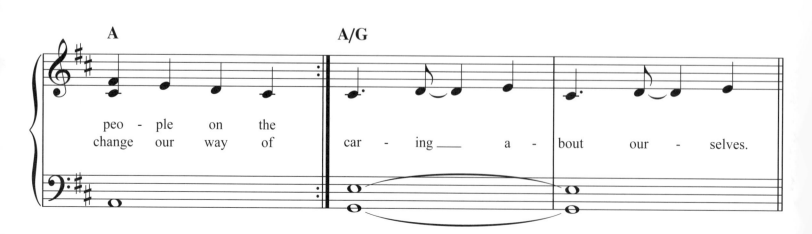

This is ____ our last dance. ____ This is ____ our -

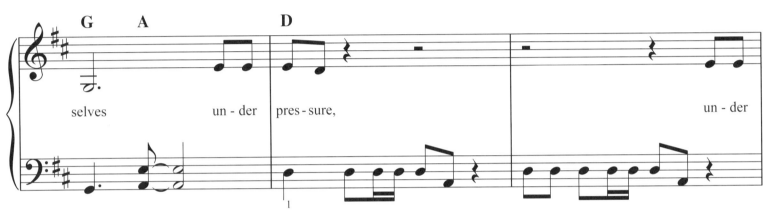

selves un - der pres - sure, un - der

pres - sure, pres - sure.

*(snap fingers)*

# WE ARE THE CHAMPIONS

Words and Music by
FREDDIE MERCURY

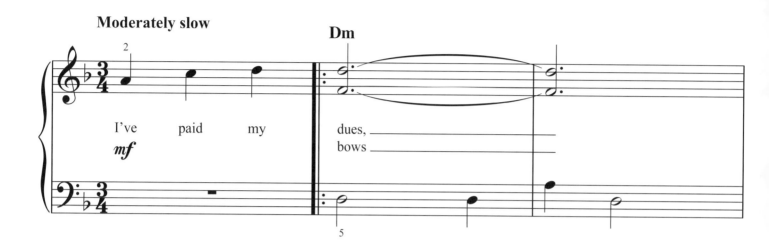

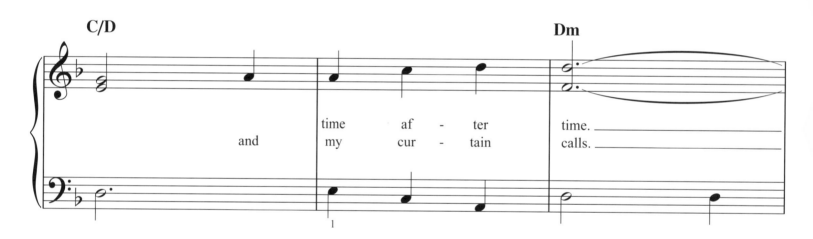

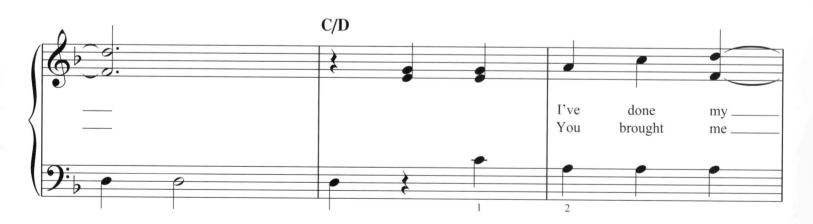

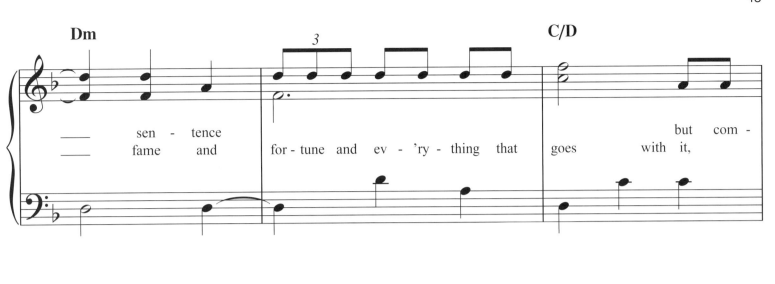

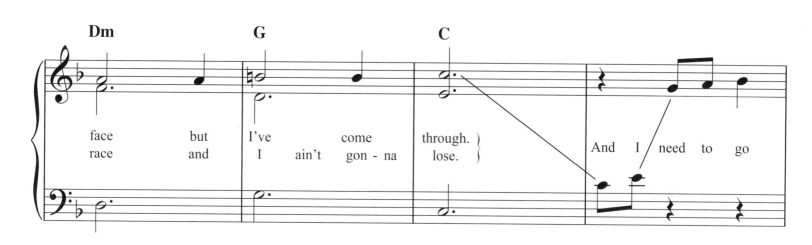

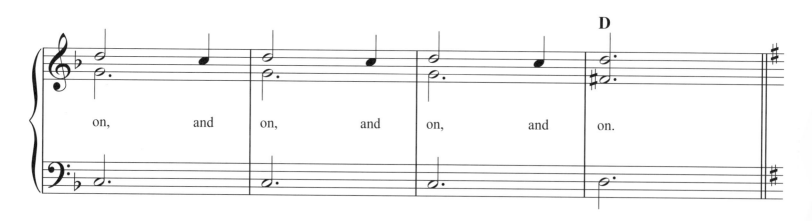

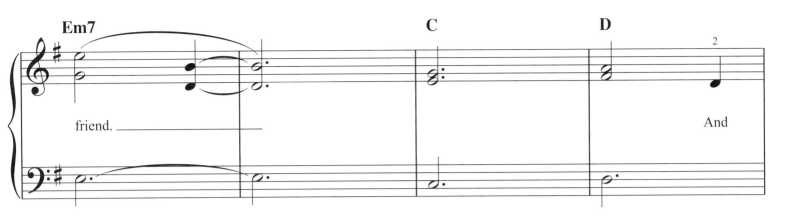

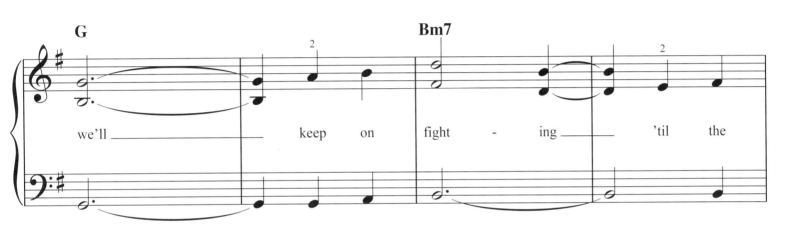

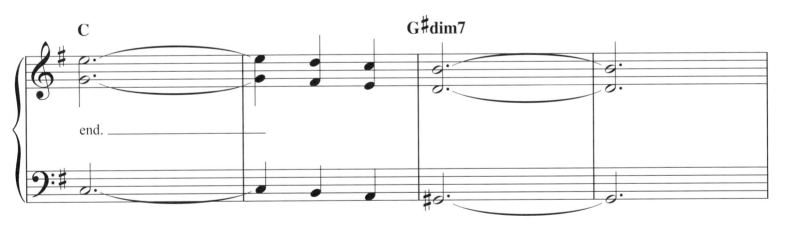

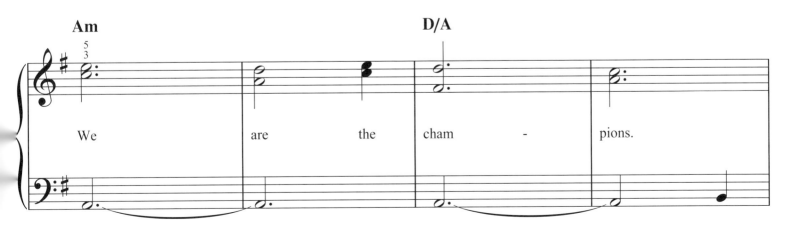

**Cdim7**

We are the cham - pions.

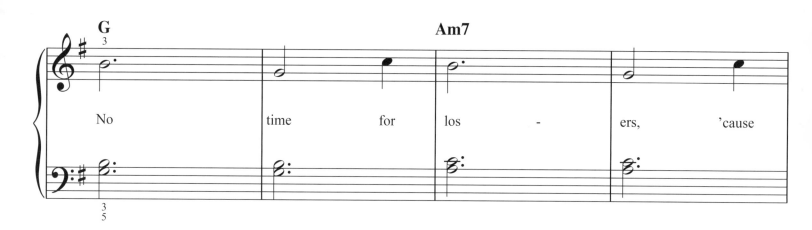

**G** **Am7**

No time for los - ers, 'cause

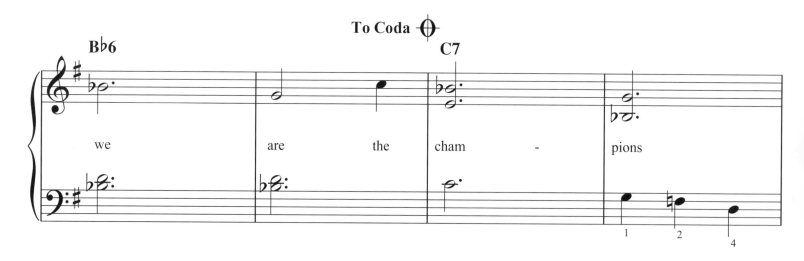

**To Coda** ⊕

**Bb6** **C7**

we are the cham - pions

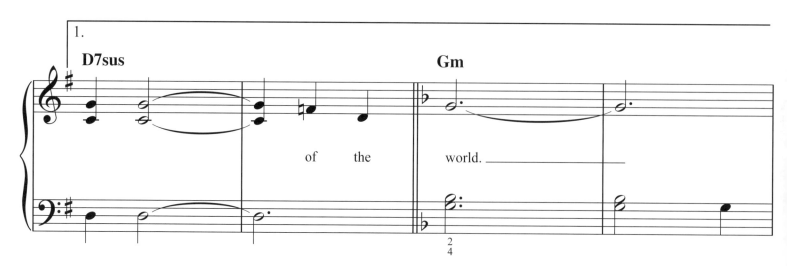

**1.**

**D7sus** **Gm**

of the world. _____

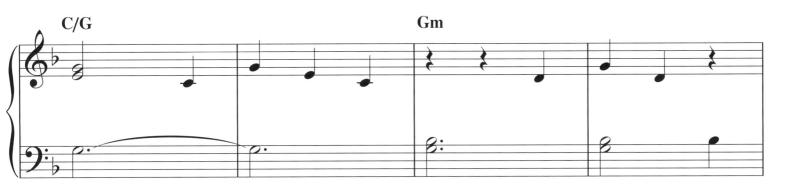

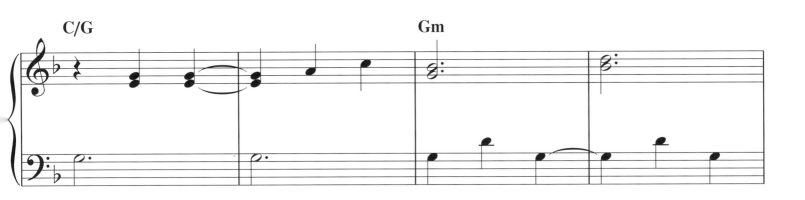

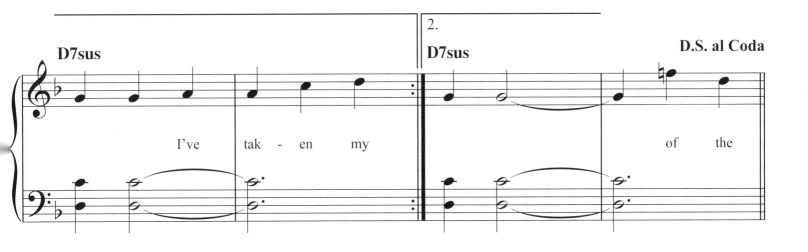

I've tak - en my

of the

cham - pions.

# YOU'RE MY BEST FRIEND

Words and Music by
JOHN DEACON

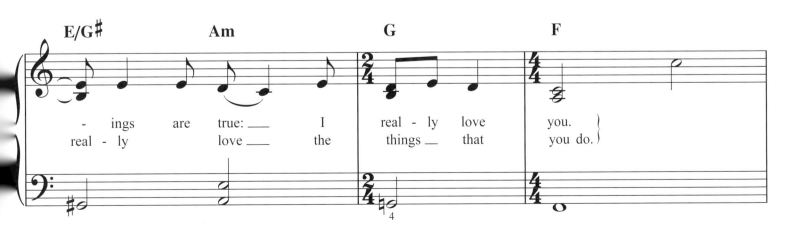

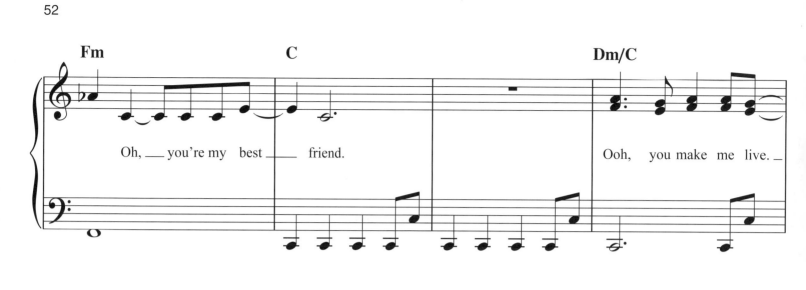

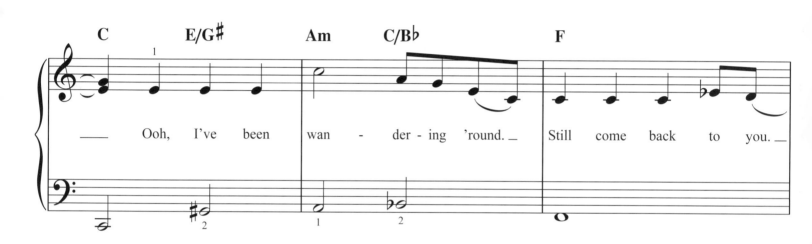

# WE WILL ROCK YOU

Words and Music by
BRIAN MAY

**Moderately**

Bud - dy, you're a boy, make a big noise play - in' in the
Bud - dy, you're a young man, hard man shout - in' in the
Bud - dy, you're an old man, poor man plead - in' with your

street. Gon - na be a big man some - day. You got
street. Gon - na take on the world some - day. You got
eyes. Gon - na make you some peace some - day. You got

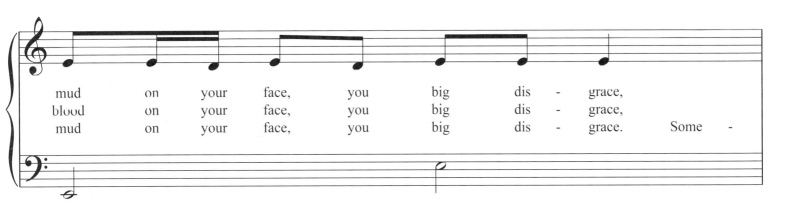

mud on your face, you big dis - grace,
blood on your face, you big dis - grace,
mud on your face, you big dis - grace. Some -

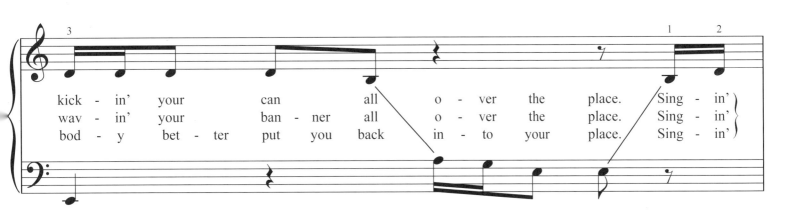

kick - in' your can all o - ver the place. Sing - in'
wav - in' your ban - ner all o - ver the place. Sing - in'
bod - y bet - ter put you back in - to your place. Sing - in'

we will, we will rock you. _____ We will, we will

rock you. _____ We will, we will rock you. _____

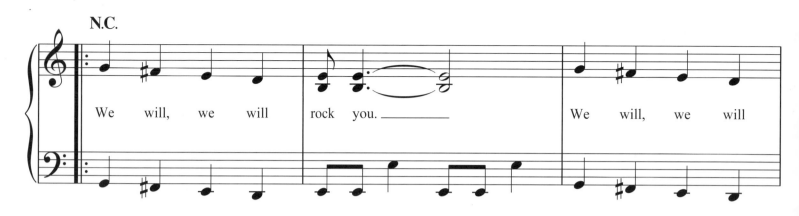

We will, we will rock you. _____ We will, we will

rock you. _____